Such a wistful - interesting face -.

The
Cheerful Cherub

by
Rebecca McCann

NEW YORK
COVICI, FRIEDE INC.
1928

Printed in the United States of America

To EVERYBODY
who reads the
Cheerful Cherub
especially
my MOTHER

By Way of Preface

ᕙ

Author to Publisher: Your letter asking me how I happened to create the Cheerful Cherub sort of paralyzes my mind because everyone I have ever met has asked me that and I never know what to say. I'll just tell you everything I can think of about him and maybe you will find something you can use for the book.

As a matter of fact I didn't really create him at all. He just came into my mind and there he stayed. I used to draw him in the margins of my school books, and I still have a bad habit of drawing him all over everything. I also used to write verses all over my school books. The way I first connected the Cherub with the verses was this:

One summer I was out in the country resting from a strenuous first year at the Academy of Fine Arts in Chicago. I used to lie out on the ground for hours, soaking up happiness from the sun and the earth, and since I was happy I wrote cheerful verses. The little Cherub smiling on the page seemed to go with the smiling verses so I used him to illustrate them. The next September (it was in 1914 so the Cherub began with the war, a nice time for me to begin my career of professional rejoicing) I went to The Chicago Evening Post carrying a huge portfolio of all my school work, and bearding an editor in his den I asked for a job.

The editor was Mr. Mason. He noticed the Cheerful Cherub verses and drawings much more than the school drawings with which I expected to demonstrate my genius. In fact he hired me with the understanding that I was to furnish a Cherub a day. So you see the Cherub got me my first job. And although I had always expected to be an artist I began work as a sort of versifier and have been one ever since. A few months after the Cherub began on the Post I had a chance to syndicate him and then the Post kept on using him from the syndicate.

The way I write the Cherub is to carry a notebook around with me and catch a verse here and there on the wing. Friends of mine who don't see me very often say they can tell what I am doing by reading the Cherub. It is a much more painless way of working, I think, to mix work with living like that instead of having regular hours for it. The only trouble is that I keep losing books of verses, leaving them on trains and mountains and places. If anyone has found one please return and get a large reward (adv.).

I can't seem to think of any Cherub anecdotes. He gets letters from readers, and every Christmas some readers send him presents. A few years ago at a studio tea in New York a very serious woman rushed up to me and said, "Are you the author of Cheerful Cherub? Well, last spring you saved me from committing suicide!" I was appalled because I never thought anyone took him really seriously.

The Cherub is also used in a school book, Robbins' and Row's Studies in English, Book One. He is right across the page from Whittier!

Of course in one way it has been a terrible thing to have had to bear the stigma of being cheerful all these years. There is an exasperating, blind and feelingless kind of cheerfulness which has been commercialized to such an extent that all cheerfulness is more or less in disrepute. I don't want the Cherub to be that way. I am certainly not that way in my private life. I am often quite gloomy, I am happy to say. The kind of cheerfulness the Cherub is supposed to believe in is really nothing but being interested in living. And interested in the little daily things, the pretty little surfaces and colors and sounds which we clump past so unseeingly because there are so many of them. I don't want him to burble life is all good regardless of other people's troubles. Because as a matter of fact I think that life is often pretty awful, and so does he. But I do want him to be a good sport and not to take himself too seriously, to keep a proper perspective on his own troubles by always being an audience of life as a whole as well as an actor in it.

This is beginning to sound pretty pompous for anything as small as the Cherub. He really hasn't any hidebound philosophy. He just goes along making little notes of the funny and happy and human and exasperating things that happen every day, and always feeling secretly surprised that he is printed.

And speaking of printing . . . some place in the book I want to acknowledge my indebtedness to George Matthew Adams, who is largely responsible for the Cherub's being printed so much. Mr. Adams has syndicated him for years, and both the Cherub and I have had so many reasons to be grateful for his friendship and encouragement, ever since the first day we appeared in his office, that we are glad to have a chance to say an enthusiastic "thank you" to him now.

Yours truly,

REBECCA McCANN

Contents

Contents--Cont.

Contents--Cont.

Contents--Cont.

Contents--Cont.

Cheerful Cherub

HURDY-GURDY

I have a hurdy-gurdy
   mind
That grinds out verse
   on this and that.
Come rain or shine I
   never stop—
I'd like a
   penny in
   my hat.

CRIMES

Of all the many crimes
My wicked past
    bestrewing
I most regret
    the ones
That some one
    caught me
    doing.

HUMANE THOUGHT

Be kind to all dumb
   animals
And give small birds
   a crumb.
Be kind to human
   beings too—
They're sometimes
   pretty dumb.

But they - so seldom appreciate
ones kindness (?)

♡ NEW LOVE 💘

Some new love should
    take the place
Of every love
    departed —
For sorrow cannot
    fill your heart
Unless you're
    hollow-hearted.

Quite true—
being fickle
is safest—

DUTY

Now duty is a horrid
  word.
Right-doing should
  be glad—
If you do good
  because you should
You might
  as well
  be bad.

FRIENDS

We're here so short
    a time before
We go to unknown
    ends.
We may not meet
    in other worlds—
Let's hurry and
be friends.

✗ NERVES ✗

I swear that I'll
  relax today.
My nerves are
  simply overtaxed—
Right now I'm all
  worked up and tense
I'm trying so to be
  relaxed.

PEBBLES

Some people say the
  whole wide world is sad
Because their own small
thoughts are cross or blue
And yet you cannot say
  the road is bad
Because you have
  a pebble in
  your shoe.

QUARREL

To keep up a quarrel
Is simply absurd
For nobody ever
Has said the last
  word.

* ✩ * KISS ☽ *

I made the nicest
  kiss I could
And blew it to the
  moon so far,
And then I watched
the empty sky
And pop—
  out came a
  little star!

MOSQUITOES

God made the star-
hung skies for us,
And singing trees and
hills and lakes.
Of course He made
mosquitoes too —
But everybody
makes
mistakes.

DISCONTENT

Contentment is a
    priceless gift,
But discontent is
    helpful too —
I want the first for
    what I have,
The second, though,
 for what
    I do.

RECIPROCATION

Look on things with
  friendly eyes,
Cast out little hates.
Just love life with
  all your heart —
Life reciprocates.

IDEAL

I fall so short of my
    ideal
At times I'm almost
    moved to cry:
"Don't judge me, please,
    by what I do —
This small cross
    person
    isn't I!"

JANUARIES

Each year I swear I'll
  keep a diary.
It's sad my resolutions
  never last—
To read them you might
  think I'd only had
A bunch of Januaries
  in my past!

❧ TRUE LOVE ❧

I don't pretend that
  life's all good,
That Nature's always
  sweet and kind.
I love the world
  the way it is——
The truest love is
never blind.

☙ DISGRACE ☙

I'd rather be the
   lowly soul
Who suffers every
   deep disgrace
Than wear that sly
   rejoicing look
That sometimes lights
   a righteous
   face.

BOREDOM

I wish I had a ticket
   for Siam.
I'm getting pretty bored
   with where I am—
But when I'm in Siam
   why all I'll do
Is wish I had a ticket
   for Peru.

BETRAYAL

I'm always caught in
  telling fibs .
I have an honest
  face, forsooth — *never!*
The while my heart is
  black with lies
My simple
  features tell
  the truth!

OPTION

Though the world is at
times a troublous place
And often my life seems
dull and drear
When I think I could
leave if I wanted to
I always begin to
like it here.

REFLECTION

Sometimes I see my life
   with such calm eyes,
Withdrawn and far
   beyond,
The way the moon looks
   down and sees a moon
Wave-broken
   on a pond.

EMPTINESS ♡

The ones who seek
  their happiness
By buying cars and
  clothes and rings
Don't seem to know
  that empty lives
Are just as empty
  filled with
  things.

FISH

A fish seems very
  sad to me —
No matter what its
  trouble
It opens up its
  mouth to moan,
And just emits
  a bubble.

GUEST

Speak gently to the
    dinner guest,
Nor chide him when
    he's late,
For some time you
    yourself may be
In his
    unhappy
    state.

RABBIT

Across the moonlight
  on the snow
I saw a young, wild
  rabbit go
How lightly! — making
  no more sound
Than his long
  shadow on
  the ground.

CERTAINTY

Though life is most
    uncertain
I'm sure of this one
    thing —
That when I'm in the
    bath tub
The telephone
    will ring.

JOYS

I love the little joys
of life —
The smell of rain,
the sound of brooks,
The taste of crispy
toast and jam,
The sight of rows
and rows
of books.

✪ STAR ✪

A star was shining in
  a well.
I let the pail down
  slow and far.
It broke the light to
  little bits — ✪
But once I
 almost had
  a star!

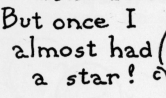

HIDDEN LIFE

I love to tell my
   secrets.
I do it all unbidden.
My hidden life's so
   thrilling
I cannot keep it
   hidden.

many of us have much thills of the past too!

PIRATES

Conversational pirates
Have caused me many
   a groan —
They hear a
   witticism
And use it as their
   own.

ONE WAY

One way I have to
baffle woe
When failure follows
all I've tried—
I suddenly detach
myself
And just sit still and
let things
slide.

❧ DETACHMENT ❧

A detached point of view
   is a wonderful thing
For it doesn't detach one
   from others.
The less I'm wrapped up
   in my personal life
The closer I get to
   my brother's.

COMMON SENSE

Common sense is
   good to have
But never let it
   master you —
For then it might
   deprive you of
The foolish
   things it's
fun to do.

GLOOM

How strange a place
  and remote from life
Is the dentist's
  reception room,
With its magazines
  that are ages old
And its feeling of
  timeless gloom!

MINOR JOY

One minor joy I have
   in fall
Almost too small to
   speak about —
It's after rain to
   step on leaves
And see the
   water
   spurting out.

UP & DOWN

The water flows now
  high, now low,
While forging onward
  with a will.
Thus life should have
now joy, now woe—
For only
stagnant pools
are still.

WASTE

I've wasted many
    precious days,
A thought that fills
    me with distress —
Stretched end to end
    they'd make a line
To reach from
    here to bright
    success.

DESKS

I wish I had a row
  of desks
Extending endlessly
  away,
For then I'd never
  clean them up —
I'd use a new one
  every day.

📖 OPEN BOOK 📖

I can't conceal my
    crimes.
I'm really quite
    distressed —
My life's an open
    book
That ought
    to be
suppressed!

PICKLES

Though life has bitter
   little times
They're not a total
   loss I feel
For mixed with joys
   they play the part
Of sour pickles
   at a meal.

SCENERY

I love our mountains
    in the west ,
So still and strange
    and tall .
I brag about our
    scenery —
You'd think
    I made
    it all .

⌒ DIARIES ⌒

The humble part I play
   in life
Does not much help my
   self-esteem—
But in the diary I
   keep
You'd be surprised
   how grand
    I seem.

DISCOVERY

I found a way to
  cure today
That foolish mood of
  hurry —
I simply stopped the
  clock and then
I didn't have
to worry.

FACES

We'd find each face
    was beautiful,
However plain it seems,
If, looking past the
    dull outside,
We saw the wistful
    dreams.

CAKE

You cannot eat your
    cake and have it .
So the cautious wise
    ones wail .
But I shall eat mine
    willy-nilly ——,
Otherwise it
    might get
    stale .

AIR

In gloomy moods it's
  never wise
To sit at home and
  mope.
Go out and take a
  long brisk walk—
Fresh air creates
  fresh hope.

DUST

I love the world —
  when die I must
Beside a road I want
  to lie
And feel upon my
  grave the dust
Of life
  forever
passing by.

BLESSINGS

They say our hardships
    help us grow
And make us strong
    and wise,
But if there's one
    thing I dislike
It's blessings
    in disguise.

READING

Reading is my
    greatest joy.
Its pleasures never
    pale —
My favorite form
    of literature
Is ads of farms
    for sale.

ABHORRENCE

Among the contraptions
My nature abhors
Are bookcases shaky,
With sticky glass
doors.

LIGHT WORDS

Words fall as lightly
   as snow.
They're easily,
   thoughtlessly said—
Yet hard words can
   enter the heart
And lie there
  as heavy
  as lead.

MOON

The moon who used to
  thrill me so
Has lost her youthful
  spell—
I never thought when
  I grew old
That she'd
  grow old
  as well.

MEALS

The meals that stretch
  all down my life
Appall me when I
  look ahead —
The lakes of soup and
  hills of meat
I'll have to eat before
  I'm dead!

RADICAL VIEWS

I really hold radical
  views about life.
Convention bars progress
  I very well know.
I always decide things
  with untrammeled mind—
I'm too nice to
live up to my
principles
though.

🖾 LOCUSTS 🖾

The locusts have a
   rasping call.
They saw the air
   with sound —
The drowsy summer
   minutes fall
In tatters to the
   ground.

COWARDICE

Although I'm brave
   enough, I'm sure,
To meet life's gravest
   situations
I lack the courage to
   refuse
My dull friends' dinner
   invitations.

VIEWS

Other people's lives
  look strange to me.
I often wonder what
  they're all about.
The only view of any
  life that's clear,
I think, is from
  the inside
looking out.

✿ MODERATION ✿

I mustn't live too
    greedily —
I'll make each
    small joy last,
And not weigh down
   my future with
An undigested
    past.

JAM

When your day gets in
   a jam
With twice the work for
   which you've time
Desert it for a
   matinee —
It's on the
way to one
that I'm!

⸮ **REGRET** ⸮

Through fear of taking
    risks in life
I've missed a lot of
    fun—
The only things that
    I regret
Are those I haven't
    done.

FOAM

The tide of summer
    rising,
A green wave strong
    and dark,
Breaks in a foam of
    blossoms
And children
    in the park.

CONTENTMENT

Well, here I sit, a
    little thing,
Contented in the sun,
And think how warm
    and gay life is,
What though it soon
    is done.

GENERATIONS

Oh, do you remember, a
   few years ago
That young generation
   that worried us so?
Well, now they are aging
   and settled, poor things—
Be calm, worried critics,
   for Time clips
   all wings.

ALAS!

I'd like to be most
    tolerant
Of all that others do
    and say,
The while I sternly
    judge myself —
Alas, I'm just the
    other way!

CHANGE

If you feel you need
   a change
I know a simple
   thing to do —
Shut your eyes, then
   open them
And take a
   different
point of
   view.

☝CONSCIENCE☝

Sometimes at night
   my conscience wakes
With pangs it seems
   that naught can lull.
If I could always
   feel like this
How good I'd be,
   and oh,
how dull!

DISTANCE

Although there's beauty
 near at hand
To distant lands my
 dreams all stray.
I see the loveliness
 of home
Most clearly
 when I'm
 far away.

TALKERS

The past is like a
    fading cloud—
We huddle on the
    future's brink,
Surrounded by
    eternity,
And tell each other
    what we think.

R. McCANN

♡ ME ♡

I feel so thrillingly
  alive
And filled with vim
  and glee
It's strange to think
  that years ago
There wasn't
  any me!

HOUSE CLEANING

We clean our houses
   every day
And throw the
   useless things away,
But often let our
   minds for years
Get filled
   with foolish
   thoughts
   and fears.

FAULTS

The faults of my
   friends
Which I freely
   condone
Are always the ones
Which resemble
   my own.

BREEZE

How sweet and brief
  the summer is!
She loves the world
  but never lingers —
I hold my hands up to
  the breeze
And feel the day run
  through
  my fingers.

BUTTERFLY

The butterfly just
  floats through life
As careless as a
  bubble.
I walk a stern and
  moral path—
A soul is
lots of
trouble.

❀ MEEKNESS ❀

I'm sure I have a
  brave stern soul
That naught in life
  can override —
But when I meet folks
  on the walk
It's always me
  who turns
  aside

GOAL

I searched the world
   for happiness
But sorrows met me
   everywhere.
They drove me back
   to my own heart—
And happiness was
   waiting there.

PAST.

I'll live each moment
to the full,
For though they soon
are gone,
Piled up they'll make
me quite a past
To build my
future on.

✐ OPERATION ✐

I've lost a sympathetic
    friend.
She underwent an
    operation —
She lived, but just to
    talk about
Insides in
    all her
conversation.

MORALS

I envy movie heroes
   bold
And large-eyed heroines
   as well.
They know so clearly
   right from wrong—
A thing I often
   cannot tell.

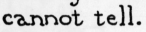

IMPORTANCE

I'm always losing
    rubbers
And breaking package
    strings —
Oh, the horrible
    importance
Of unimportant
    things.

☞ EXERCISE ☞

My road through life
    is rough at times,
With hills that dip
    and rise.
But this all helps my
    character —
It needs the
    exercise.

Well – it gets plenty!

〖 80 〗

❦ ONE FRIEND ❦

Don't try to flee your
   loneliness .
You'll only find it in
   the end .
Just get acquainted
   with yourself —
You'll gain one
understanding
   friend .

✎ DECISION ✎

Whenever a problem
   comes up in my life
I decide it and
   promptly forget it—
It isn't so much the
   decision that counts
As the will power not
   to regret it.

Learn!

THRILL

I went out to a well
  one night.
Soft darkness hid
  all daytime scars.
I held some water to
  the light
And drank a
dipper full
of stars.

MENDING

When clouds are dark
  just get to work.
You'll never help by
  whining —
A stitch in time, I
  always say.,
Will mend a
  silver lining.

SECRETS

When people tell me
   secrets
I'm often moved to ?
  ask
Since they themselves
  can't keep them
Why give to me
  that task.

BY-PRODUCT

Among my many long
    dead loves
Which now look flat
    and foolish
I prowl and poke for
    things to write —
It seems a little
    ghoulish.

HIGHER THINGS

I sort of flounder
  through my days,
Losing money, missing
  cars —
I keep my mind on
  higher things
And thus I
  get some
  awful jars.

CAT

I fuss and chatter
    through the day.
I sew, I read a silly
    book.
The cat who lies and
    thinks for hours
Just gave me
    one long
weary look.

BILLS

We have to pay for
   everything.
Each reckless joy the
   spirit wills
Goes past — and then
   along comes life
Relentlessly collecting
   bills.

YAWNS

I'm yawning from
  morning till night.
It's awful the hours
  I keep —
I simply can't live
  long enough,
I'm afraid, to catch up
  on my sleep.

BABIES

Babies reach for
   anything
That's glittering to
   see —
And though I'm old I
   sometimes think
It's just the
   same with
   me.

:☀: SYMPATHY :☀:

Sympathy by all is
needed.
Freely ought we all
to give it —
No one knows how
hard a life is
But the one who has
to live it.

STAMPS

With all my hard-
    earned cash
Most recklessly I
    part
But when I waste
    a stamp
It simply
    breaks my
    heart.

LAUGH

I'm often more clever
  and catty than kind
It's such a temptation
  to show off my mind,
But if to gain laughter
  I hurt a good friend
It's plain that the laugh
  is on me
  in the end.

OUR WORLD

The moon is a queen who
 walks lovely and mute,
The sun is majestic
 and golden and high,
The stars are like notes
 on a heavenly flute —
But our world is the
 funniest thing
 in the sky.

~❧ OBJECTION ☙~

These books on "How to
   Win Success"
Have left my problems
   all unsolved —
They sound inspiring,
   but I find
There's always too
   much work
   involved.

LADIES

How smooth and pleasant
   ladies are!
Their surfaces are
   never changed
Unless they hear a
   shocking truth
And get their
   features
   disarranged.

some people—

TOLERANCE

I sternly judge my
  fellow men
When I've been
  righteous for a while —
But when I've not,
  broad-mindedly
  give their faults
  a tolerant
  smile.

FIRMNESS

Firm I stand through
   storm and stress.
I know that it will
   end.
I will not break
   beneath my woe—
But goodness,
   how I bend!

TACTLESSNESS

The moon is kind to
  lovers,
None friendlier than
  she —
But to the lonely-
  hearted
How tactless
  she can be!

STONE

I'd like to buy a
   diamond ring—
I pay my board
   instead.
Alas, I ask of life
   a stone
And all I get
   is bread!

MY ACTS

I will not let my
    grievous past
With vain remorse
    torment me —
I can't help feeling
    that my acts
Don't really
    represent me.

SPLASH

I love goloshes and
  slickers so,
Their names sort of
  splash together.
I flop and slip through
  the sloppy snow —
Oh, how I
  enjoy bad
  weather!

TACT

When you've made an
    awful blunder
Don't bewail your
    brainless act —
Think of all your past
    successes,
Show yourself a
    little tact.

✝ AFFLICTION ♛

The members of our
    human race
Who move me most
    to scornful diction
Are sensitive and
    injured souls
Luxuriating in
    affliction.

THOUGHT

My work just worried
   me today
So that I couldn't do
   my best
Until I had this lovely
   thought :
The world can stand
   it if I rest.

FEET

The price of shoes has
  spoiled my life
Which once was calm
  and sweet —
Although I slave the
  livelong day
I cant support
  my feet!

INTERRUPTIONS

Interruptions steal
  my time,
And callers make me
  run and hide —
When I am in the
  mood to work
I want the world to
  stand aside.

BIRDS

Birds that perch on
  fence and tree
Glance uncuriously
  at me,
Not caring, as they
  take my crumb,
Where I go,
  or whence
I come.

CRIME

Some people speak
    of killing time.
I don't know any
    greater crime.
With work and beauty
    they might fill it—
And yet they sit
    around and
        kill it.

SOULS

Through war and
  suffering and woe
To ever distant goals
All bravely forging
  on alone
We steer our little
  souls.

⊞ WINDOWS ⊞

The whole world looks
a dreary place
When through soiled
windows it is seen.
A lesson this should be
to us
To keep our
mental
windows
clean.

♀ APPEARANCES ♀

Misleading are
    appearances.
One's true self is
    within —
A corpulent outside
    may hide
A soul that's starved
and thin.

CONFESSION

Although I'm often
   foolish
And my life is full
   of breaks
I make a sort of
   virtue
Of admitting
   my mistakes.

✠ SOLUTION ✠

I had a problem in
 my life.
I pondered on it
 filled with care.
But once I'd gathered
 all the facts
I saw the problem
 wasn't there.

BABBLERS

Hundreds of people
    paint pictures,
Hundreds write verses
    like me —
Hundreds of brooklets
    that babble
Are lost in the depths
    of the sea!

⚖ RULES ⚖

Conventions cramp my
  sweeping style.
Why should I be
  ruled by custom?
Rules were only
  made, I think,
For those
  who are too
  weak to
   bust 'em.

♪♩♪ MUSIC ♪♩♪

I'd like to go where
  music grows —
While violin notes
  blew my hair
I'd wander through
  the organ groves
And gather little
  grace notes
    there.

PRESENT

This moment is the
　　peak of time.
On it we stand and
　　we can see
The future and the
　　past stretch out,
Two roads
to one
eternity.

ACCEPTANCE

We live the most when
    we accept
Most fully what the
    days reveal,
For life is only, in
    itself,
An opportunity to
    feel.

⚬•⚬ HOPE ⚬•⚬

My hope springs up
   in spite of blows,
Higher after every
   fall.
Down the road of
   life it goes
Bounding like
   a rubber
   ball.

☾ MOONLIGHT ☆

The moon gets all
 its brightness
From the sun's reflected
 rays.
That's why its light
 is eerie —
It's made
 of ghosts
 of days.

.∞. MOTORING .∞.

I have a little flivver
That goes up and down
   with me ,
And how we stay
   together so
Is more than I
   can see.

Emma

♀ OPINION ♀

What people might think
shall not govern my life
Whatever I want I
    will dare .
I'm a slave to opinion
    though nevertheless —
I want them to know
I don't care.

GAME

Well, life may not have
    much meaning.
Blind chance seems to
    rule each day —
But if you can take
    it lightly
It's a pretty
    good game
    to play.

BUGS

I love the little
    cheerful bugs
That chirp and sing
    all summer long.
The summer days are
    strung like beads
Upon their fine
unbroken song.

✄ REPENTANCE ✄

I like to feel repentant when
    when
I haven't done the
    things I should—
It makes me feel
    more virtuous
Than if I'd kept on
being good!

GOATS

How I feel for those
  goats in the mountains
Who leap over canyons
  all day !
I go leaping from
  pay day to pay day
The same insecure-
  feeling way.

AIM

I do not aim for
wealth or fame.
I've other hope than
    that —
I long to find before
    I die
Just one
becoming
hat.

RAINBOW

A pot of gold you're
    sure to find
If to the rainbow's
    end you go —
The man who has a
    pot of gold
Can't always find
    a rainbow
    though.

❧ WEAKNESS ❧

Life was given me to
   use,
But when it makes
   me tired or blue
I'm letting it use me   *Sure!*
   instead —
And that's a foolish
   thing to do.

JOB

If your job is <u>work</u>
to you
Quit it, I am here
to say —
Find the work you're
meant to do
And it won't
be work
but play.

✕ TWO LIVES ✕

Because time goes
   too fast for me
I can't do half the
   things I ought —
I have two lives,
   the one I act
And one I only live
   in thought.

PETALS

The sun is just a
   flower gay
That blooms above us
   very high,
And every fragrant,
   soft-aired day
A petal falling from
   the sky.

♪ CONCERT ♪

My hearts always soothed
  by sweet music
When life seems quite
  hopeless and bad.
It's not that it makes
  me feel happy —
It makes me
  enjoy feeling
  sad.

GOLF

I'm taking up the game
   of golf—
I use my mashie with
   such force
I heard a catty person
   say
I'm also
taking up
the course.

⚜ OLD AGE ⚜

There is no such thing
  as old age I believe.
In the long race with time I
am sure we're all winning.
The closer we draw to
  the end of things here
The nearer we are to *where?*
  some other
beginning.

💰 SUCCESS 💰

To get ahead is not
    success.
Progressive men, I
    often find,
Have hurried so for
    worldly wealth
That they have left
    their souls
    behind.

? QUESTION ?

There's a question that's
always in my mind;
It bothers me and will
not cease —
Is it better to be a
grabby child
Or always take the
smallest
piece?

🎻 TUNING-UP 🎻

I heard musicians
    tuning up,
And thought, "The
    discord and the strife
That seem to fill my
    days right now
Are just the tuning-up
    for life."

HOARDING

If you hoard your
    wealth of course
You'll have it for a
    rainy day,
But if you hoard your
    love you'll find
That it has
    vanished
all away.

WALL

Selfishness is like a
    wall,
A useless wall, without
    a doubt —
It cannot hold my
    own joy in
But only keeps the
    world's joy out.

ꙮ TOMORROW ꙮ

Cheerily my way
    I go.
To sorrow I'm
    inured.
I had it once and
    now I know
Tomorrow it
    is cured.

GAIN

They say that youth's
the care-free time
But I have learned
with age this truth:
It's just by growing
old we gain
The wisdom to enjoy
our youth.

❡SURROUNDINGS❡

I wish I had a
    different house,
With slides instead
    of stairs
And springboards on
    the landings too
And cushions
    everywheres.

EXCUSES

I can always make
  excuses
When I'm disinclined
  to work
But when I am hiring
  some one
How I hate to see
  him shirk !

ꭍ FOOTPRINTS ꭍ

I love a field of
  smooth clean snow
Untouched by any
  human feet.
And when I have to
  walk through one
I try to make
  my footprints
  neat.

APOLOGY

If this cheerfulness
  annoys you
On the days you're
  feeling blue
Please forgive me,
  gentle reader—
Often it annoys me too.

TRAVEL

Though travel is
    confusing
With burdens far from
    light,
By simply looking
    helpless
I get along
    all right.

MEDES

I hear of the Medes
  and Persians
But never pay much
  heed —
I don't believe I
  could mention
A single, prominent
  Mede !

✿ LIFE ✿

Life is very simple.
We dress in cloth
   and leather,
And laugh and cry
   a little
Among a lot of
   weather.

MANNERS

At parties although I am
  bitterly bored
I act just as pleased as
  I can all the while —
And so when the world
  hands me sorrowful
  times
I ought to
remember my
manners,
and smile.

JUSTICE

I'd rather be mean
 to a person
Than mean to a dog
 or a cat,
For people can tell
 a policeman
And animals cannot
 do that.

GIFTS

I want all kinds of
  feelings in my life.
We gain from all our
  joys and sufferings.
Contentment gives us
  health and beauty too,
And courage is the gift
  that sorrow
  brings.

POOL

I can't roam freely
  through the world,
Life seems to shut
  me in with bars;
And yet a pool that
  lies quite still
Can mirror flying birds
  and stars.

GOSSIP

I heard some talk
   about myself,
And most unfair it
   seemed to be —
Oh, well, I live in my
   own mind
And not in others'
   thoughts
   of me.

☼PREFERENCE☼

I much prefer a
person
With a black heart
underneath
To some pure soul who
sniffles
Or whistles
through his
teeth.

"MOTH"

A moth is such a
  fairy thing,
So lightly through
  the air it floats —
Who'd think that it
  subsisted on
Our heavy winter
  overcoats!

❀ TALENT ❀

I'll never have the
    fortune
Which only genius
    brings
But I have a lot of
    talent
For enjoying little
    things.

⏰ LACK ⏰

The human race varies
in marvelous ways.
We are clever and
foolish and deep.
In only one thing we're
alike it would seem—
We never have had
enough sleep.

❡ QUERY ?

They say a life of
  struggle grim,
Of facing every
  task,
Will get you some
  place in the end —
But where,
  if I may
  ask ?

Where — yes — where!

▣ DOOR ▣

A door is so adaptable,
It leads to spaces
        wide,
Or when you want
   to be alone
It shuts
   the world
   outside.

HORIZONS

"When I get rich" the
   children dream
With eyes on some
   far day.
And when they're old,
   with eyes turned back:
"When I was rich"
   they say.

📖 STUDY 📖

We study a trade or
  profession for years
Before we can hope
  for success —
And yet though we want
to have lives full of joy
We all study living
  much less.

MILLIONAIRES

I never envy
      millionaires
Their wealth and
    motor cars —
I'd like to be a poet
   though
For they
own all
the stars.

*Think with a few
millions I could
better enjoy the
stars —*

⚬𝒸𝒹⚬ **SLEEP** ⚬𝒸𝒹⚬

The night makes
   people more united.
While awake they're
   far asunder,
But sleep is like a
   warm, grey blanket
All of us can huddle
   under.

❧ IMPULSE ❧

I'd like to hug the
   human race
So much I feel that I
   adore it
But if I tried this on
   the street
I s'pose I'd
  get arrested
  for it.

♟ SHADOWS ♟

Shadows in the noon-
   day sun are sharp;
At sunset they are long
   and soft and still.
So troubles that are black
   and hard in youth
Grow soft with age—
   at least I think
   they will.

FENCES

When I consider Time
  and Space
It fills me with a
  quiet mirth
To see a human
  fencing off
A tiny portion
  of the
    earth.

TREE

I think I'd like to be a
    tree,
And stand and sway
    without a care;
And have the fragrant
    rain-washed wind
Run long, strong
    fingers
through my
    hair.

SHAPES

While animals live
    care-free lives
And birds soar high on
    joyous wings
The human race with
    wood and nails
Just fills the world
    with shapes
of things.

DARING

I like a life of
    daring,
To make mistakes
    and then
Look forward, never
    caring,
And take
    new risks
    again.

POETS

The poets talk like
  supermen
In strange, uplifting verse.
But when you meet
  them you can see
They're just the same as
  you and me,
Or sometimes
  even worse.

🛁 CURE 🛁

I know a way to
   cure the blues
As sure as anything:
Turn on the bath tub
   water hard
And then get in and
   sing.

ADS

Among the ads in
   magazines
There lives a quaint
   and happy race,
Their problems solved
   by soap or soup,
A smile on every
   simple face.

✣ POSSESSIONS ✣

Possessions weigh me
    down in life.
I never feel quite free.
I wonder if I own
    my things
Or if my things
    own me.

ADVICE

At times you ought
  to stay alone
I make so bold as to
  advise
And just be friendly
  with your soul —
Your soul will miss
  you otherwise.

⧗ TIME ⧗

Time is such a
    mystery,
So gentle and so
    healing —
The days slip past
    like colored cards
That Father Time
    is dealing.

DRIFTING

I do not strive to
    guide my life
With firm and brain-
    restricted hand—
So often, drifting here
    and there,
I touch the
shores of
fairyland.

🐱 DUMBNESS 🐶

Dumb animals we call
 them
While they bark and
 neigh and moo.
They talk as much
 as we do —
To them we seem
 dumb too.

PANGS

Oh, how I regret in
  the night
With pangs that will
  never abate
Those brilliantly
  crushing retorts
I think of a little
  too late!

♡ OUR LIVES ♡

Our lives all
    interweave,
Each needed in its
    place.
And every heavy
    heart
Is weighing down
    the race.

PROGRESS

In my youth I set
  my goal
Farther than the eye
  could see.
I am nearer to it
  now —
I have moved
  it nearer me.

LIGHT

Stained glass windows
  make the light
Like songs of beauty
  from the sun.
Life could shine
  through _us_ like that,
You and
  me and
  everyone.

DRAMATIC INSTINCT

I've dramatized my
   life too much
I'm so poetically
   gifted.
At concerts I don't
   listen now —
I sit and try to look
   uplifted.

OUTLOOK

We can't look far
   ahead or back.
By time we're over-
   awed —
Well, since my view
   of life's not long
I'll try to
   keep it
   broad.

🐢 LEISURE 🐇

To live with leisure
   every day
And never fret or
  worry
Will make each hour
   twice as long —
No one has
  time to
   hurry.

ADJUSTMENT

To get adjusted to
   the world
Is after all the
   wisest aim.
It won't adjust itself
   to us
For it was here
   before
we came.

OPTIMISTS

Although I side with
    optimists
And think they have
    the right of it,
I'm not just glad
    because of life,
But often-times
    in spite
of it.

SMALL THINGS

I love small uncivilized
    things,
Babies and rabbits
    and birds,
Who carry around
    in their eyes
Little strange
    thoughts
without words.

☼ TRUTH ☼

Truth is the holy
    grail I seek,
Beyond all small
    ambitions.
The only truth I've
    found is this —
Truth changes
    with
conditions.

WORK

I'm glad I have to
    work to live —
I'd hate to reach my
    final day
And have a guilty
    feeling then
That I had
never paid
my way.

PLAN

We're all a part of one
   big plan
To work together,
   not compete —
Thus one who beats
   his fellow man
Has really caused his
   own defeat.

❧ YEARNING ❧

When people yearn
  with all their hearts
For just one treasure
  far away
They close their eyes
  to countless joys
That crowd
around them
  every day.
    R. M⸱CANN.

YOUTH

Youth brings the
    greatest gladness,
Or so I'm often
    told —
And I can always
    keep it
Unless my heart
    grows old.

❧ EXCEPTIONS ❧

I try to be friends with
the whole human race
And feel they're my
brothers whatever they do,
Except those at concerts
who sit next to me
And put on their
rubbers before
it's all through.

FEAR

Do the thing you're
   most afraid of ;
Never let it know you
   fear it.
Dangers only hurt
   the body
But it's fear
   that kills
the spirit.

WHISTLES

The noonday whistles'
  piercing shrieks
To me are music
    wild and sweet —
With gladsome cries
  that reach the skies
They tell the world
  it's time
  to eat.

BEES

I love it in the
  country
But one thing
  worries me —
The bees work all
  day Sunday
Which really
  shouldn't be.

VANITY

The things in life I
really want
Are all quite moderate
and wise —
The foolish things I
think I want
Are just to dazzle
others' eyes.

MAN

Although I pity ancient
man,
(We're luckier than
he),
I hate to think
posterity
Will some day
pity me!

📖 RESOLVE 📖

I let the blues creep
  in today —
I'll take possession
  of tomorrow
And cram it full of
  work and play
And not leave any
  room for
  sorrow.

☃ VIEWPOINT ☃

No other two people
  can ever have
Such different points
  of view
As the man who sub-
  lets a furnished flat
And the tenant
  he rents
  it to.

ADVENTURERS

Progress comes from
    adventurers,
Explorers of land and
    thought.
The absolute
    conservative
Gives civilization
    naught.

PRACTISE

My days are full of
    blunders —
Oh, how I've always
    yearned
To live one life for
    practise,
Another when
    I've learned!

Oh that we could!

DETAILS

I don't *see* life in
  the abstract
As something sweeping
  and grand —
I bury my head in
  its details
As an ostrich
  does in
  the sand.

☙EQUALITY☙

Of course we're free
   and equal here
In spite of fame or
   pelf.
Some seem more free
   than others though—
I'm "equaller"
   myself.

PULL

If I should get ahead
    through pull
Instead of earning
    my advance
I'd lose as much in
    character
As I'd be gaining
    in finance.

👹 SIMPLE LIFE 👹

I'd like to live a
simple life
And concentrate on
some high aim
Ignoring worldly
pomp and show,
If all my friends
would do
the same.

PRAYER

May I walk my ways
Clear-eyed and
      free
And do some good
Anonymously.

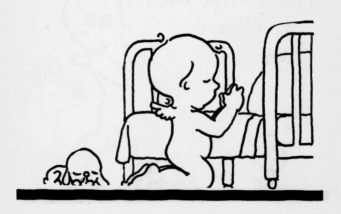

REVOLVING DOORS

Revolving doors are
    spiteful things
I cannot help but
    feel.
Unless I leap out
    breathlessly,
They nip me
    on the
    heel.

✋ CRUDITY ✋

My crude baby sister
   makes terrible breaks,
And nothing we do seems
   to stop her .
She won't be unnatural ,
   scold as we may —
And we all know that
   Nature's improper.

♨ DIGNITY ♨

I'd like to skip along
  the street
But I must walk
  with stately stride.
Who started all this
  foolishness
Of people
acting
dignified?

☼ **WIT** ☼

I think of witty
   things to say.
I'd be considered
   bright —
Except I always
   think them in
The middle of the
   night!

JOY

Life itself can't give
  me joy
Unless I really will
  it.
Life just gives me
  time and space—
It's up to me
to fill it.

and know me
fill it!

❦ LONELINESS ❧

Am I the only one in
   life
Who always seems to
   stand apart
Or is it everyone
   who feels
A little lonesome
   in his heart?

❧ LIVING ❧

Though usually I
    spend my time
By my own life
    engrossed
It's when I'm helping
    others live
I feel I'm living
    most.

ACCOMPANIMENT

Truth makes life a
    noble thing,
And courage makes
    it strong,
But grace and tact
    must set them off
As music does
    a song.

✿ KNIGHTS ✚

No more do gallant
  knights ride out
On chargers bold
  with banners gay —
But many just as
  noble knights
Charge forth
on street cars
every day.

WISDOM

The wise old writers
  left advice
On how we might
  avoid life's stings.
To heed their words
  might cure our woes —
Except they all said
  different
  things.

DOUBLE MEANING

Though words may seem
  to be direct
Their meaning often
  is twofold —
When people say,
  "How young you look!"
I realize
I'm getting
old. *Ha!*

Just as

❦ MONKEYS ❧

I stood before the
monkeys' cage,
Their funny ways
to see —
I laughed at them
a lot until
I saw one
laugh
at me.

Central Park.
N. Y.
Easter – 1943.

MISTAKES

I'd rather make
   mistakes at times,
(For even in mistakes
   I live)
Than be afraid to
   take a risk
And make my whole
   life negative.

REALITY

I look into a mirror
And doubt reality —
A shadow of a
    shadow
My face looks back
    at me.

WORDS

Words have colors
   and music
And wisdom and joy
   as well —
How lovely I think
   that words are
There are no words
   to tell!

STATUE

I love a statue old
  and still.
Ancient moods pervade
  it.
It's strange how much
  more real it is
Than the hand
  that made it.

SKY

I love the tender
    brooding sky,
It rests my eyes
    and spirit too —
I wish that I could
climb up high
And plunge my
 arms deep
 in its blue.

❧ DEMOCRACY ❧

I feel my kinship
  with the low.
They're good as I am
  any day ——
It irritates me
  quite a lot
To find that
  they too feel
  this way.

☕ MONOTONY ☕

I claim imagination,
But that's an idle
    boast
When every day
    for breakfast
I eat an egg and
    toast.

STYLE

I've lost some great
   and stylish friends.
I'm glad as I can be.
The strain of living
   up to them
Was nearly killing
   me.

WOE

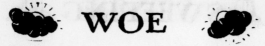

I find that woe is
   never quite
As final as I feared.
Thus as I flounder
   through my life
I feel a little
   cheered.

SWEEPING

I like to sweep the
  front porch steps;
The sun shines and the
  birds all sing.
I hate to sweep the
  kitchen floor—
I never see
or hear
a thing.

🐱 CONDUCT 🐶

A rule for good
    conduct
Which hasn't failed
    yet
Is just to do
    nothing
You'd like to forget.

Forget everything—
let conduct take care
of itself.

🪽 VIRTUE 🪽

I've worked to build
     my character.
I wish I'd not
     commenced it,
For virtue is its
     own reward—
That's what
     I have
against it.

Oh to be free!

STATESMEN

Statesmen stand in
    long black coats
And speak wise words
    from ample throats.
I always think with
    wonder then
Of how small babes
    become
    such men!

AGE

Although old age is
    creeping on
To all its troubles
    I'm resigned.
My joints may stiffen
    but I'll not
Have rheumatism in
    my mind.

FLEA

My dog presented me
  today
With just one little
  flea.
He missed it not at all,
  but, oh—
The difference
  to me!

BURGLARS

A burglar stole my
   jewelry
But that was really
   kind —
No longer now my
   jewelry
Can steal
  my peace
  of mind.

STORMS

I'd like to take my
   grief the way
A tree bends to the
   storms that beat it,
To see it as a part
   of life
And, by accepting it,
   defeat it.

✋ PALMISTRY ✋

A palmist read my
  hand today.
It filled me with
  surprise——
In spite of what
  I've always thought
It seems I'm strong
  and wise!

NAVIGATION

The sailor has no
    harder job
Who sails the stormy
    oceans
Than I who steer
    my little soul
Through
strange and
deep emotions.

🐪 CAMELS 🐪

I never think of
    camels much,
But always see them,
    when I do,
In endless caravans
    although
I 'spose they have
    their home
        life too.

WEATHER

I love grey days of
    wind and rain
When all the big trees
    shout and play,
And misty days all
    filled with dreams—
I just love
    weather
    anyway.

CHARGE ACCOUNT

I love to have a
    charge account.
It makes for painless
    buying —
Except that when the
    bills come in
My family's so
    trying.

♁UNDERSTANDING♡

Sometimes our friends
 may seem quite false
But we should still try
 not to lose them—— *of course—*
If we could see within
 their minds
It might be easy to
 excuse them.

PAY

I'm sorry that the
    world's arranged
So we must do our
    work for pay —
I always feel I
    gain the most
When I can give my
    work away.

LOSS

Bare trees against
  the winter sky
Make patterns delicate
  as lace.
Thus loss can give
  the strong of soul
A special kind
  of charm
  and grace.

a winter's twilight
at "Sea Horses"
1929-'30

SMUGNESS

I feel so smug when
    I've been good
I soon become
    unbearable —
I'm really pleasanter
    to know
When I have just been
    terrible!

✿ POLITENESS ✿

Now animals aren't
   polite ,
Each tries to outdo
  his own brother,
But we tip our hats
  when we meet
And open the
  door for
each other.

✵☀✵ 🧜 SHOW 🧜 ✵☀✵

If you think that the
   world is all wrong,
That civilization's a
   botch,
At least you will have
   to admit
It's a pretty good
   show to
   watch.

FOG

The fog comes
    creeping quietly .
A sense of mystery
    it brings,
And by half-hiding
    it reveals
More beauty
    in familiar
    things.

✿ DISCRETION ✿

I'm honest as the day
    is long,
But only through
    discretion :
I cannot tell a lie —
    I lack
Control of my
    expression.

⚡ EXPLOSION ⚡

"When everything goes
   dead wrong"
And fate presses down
   on my load,
Am I noble and brave?
No, I break things and
   rave —
It's such
  a relief
to explode.

What a relief!

CHASE

I long for a life of
more leisure.
I rush through the day,
till it feels
As if I am chasing
tomorrow
While yesterday
snaps at
my heels.

MYSTERY

Often across long
   miles of space
Strange voices speak
   strange words to me.
It brings such mystery
   to life
When central makes
  mistakes,
   you see.

♡ NEGLECT ◉

Whenever I have
 cause to feel
That life's neglecting
 me a bit
I find the only
 reason is
That I'm not giving
 much to it.

FORMALITY

I'm friends with trees
   and animals
As if I always knew
   them —
Just humans seem to
   think I need
An introduction
   to them.

 TRIMMING

The fabric of my life
  is grey —
Hard work in one
  small place.
I'll concentrate on
  trimming it
With lots of laughs
  for lace.

✂ BATHING SUITS ✂

When pompous people
    squelch me
With their regal
    attributes
It cheers me to
    imagine
How they'd look
    in bathing
    suits.

RESTING

Be lazy sometimes, I
    advise.
Don't blame yourself
    and think you shirk.
It's very wise to
    realize
That resting is a part
    of work.

♡ LOVE 💰

A man can own uncounted
 gold
And land and buildings
 tall,
But love is just to
 give away—
It can't be
owned
at all.

☼ GLADNESS ☼

When I'm sad all my sad-
ness is centered in me.
The world just as happily
passes me by.
But when I am glad all
my gladness goes out
And feels just as big
as the earth
and the sky.

AUTUMN

Youth and loves as
   light as spray
Like fragrant petals
   drift away.
Stark at last, and
   somehow freed,
Stands the stalk
   that bears
   the seed.

PRIDE

I threw my coat
around me
To take a haughty
leave,
But my hand went
through the lining
Instead of
down the
sleeve!

TROUBLE

Courage can lessen
  misfortune
To quite a surprising
  degree —
The trouble is never
  with trouble
So much as it is
  with me.

FAME

Each tries to get his
   share of fame
In spite of modest
   disavowals —
Some carve their
   names in history ,
And some embroider
   them on
   towels.

OH, WELL

I can accept the fate
  of each tomorrow.
A rootless gladness
  blooms above my sorrow.
Across my life, a field
  that bears no seed,
Go bobbing
  little joys like
  tumble-weed.

ARGUMENT

I love a good hot
    argument.
I'll talk for hours
    anywhere —
But just one rule
    must be observed:
To use statistics
    isn't fair.

EGO

In all my thoughts
how big I seem!
I stand conspicuous
in space,
While, like a chorus
on the stage,
Behind me
stands the
human race.

SHOPPING

It takes all the joy from
  a wild shopping spree
And the next day it
  drives me distraught
To find that the shops
  took me seriously
And <u>sent</u> me
the things
that I
bought!

CROWD

When I'm alone I'm just
  honestly me,
Not foolish or humble
  or proud.
But when I'm with others
  I'm acting a part—
I always
  get lost
in a crowd.

ANYWAY

I've had some awful
    illnesses
And accidents that
    stretched me flat,
But anyway I'm still
    alive —
And lots of people
    can't say that!

HURRAH

I did the thing I
    feared the most.
Excuse me while I
    cheer.
Now here I stand, a
    stronger soul —
And all I've
    lost is
    Fear.

✺ SOUL ✺

Who'd think to see
  my plodding feet
And plain though
  useful face
I have a gay and
  dancing soul
      That flits
      from place
      to place?

CHECK BOOK

I cannot keep my
   check book straight—
I find, to be quite
   frank,
I'm much too lavish
   with myself
And stingy with
   the bank.

HOUSES

We all live in houses
  of thought
Life builds in our
  minds so it seems —
The walls and the
  floors are just facts,
But the windows and
  doors are
  our dreams.

? WHY ?

Whene'er I'm in
  revolving doors
Behind a fat and
  pompous man
Why am I moved to
  spin around
As fast and
  furious as
  I can?

OCEAN

It's strange when in
a storm at sea
At which my courage
fails
To think this ocean
even now
Is home, sweet home,
to whales.

SWALLOWS

I love to watch the
   swallows soar.
With lilting rhythmic
   grace they fly,
As if a flock of small
   black notes
Were writing
   music on
   the sky.

¡INCONSISTENCY!

I'm sure I have a
   noble mind
And honesty and tact,
And no one's more
   surprised than I
To see the way
   I act!

💰 MY TIME 🕐

My possessions belong
   to my friends
But I must have it
   known,
Though freely I'd part
   with my wealth,
That my time
   is my own.

MEMORY

My memory's like a
   spider's web
That holds bright joys
   like drops of dew,
With here and there
   an awful rent
Where whole
long weeks
have fallen
through.

☀ COURAGE ☀

If you have tried and
   tried again
Nor made your effort
   less
You really have
   succeeded then—
For courage is
   success.

ECONOMY

I can't afford
  economy—
I save a dollar now
  and then
Which makes me feel
  so virtuous
I'm always moved to
  squander ten.

SHELTER

With little strict
   conventions
And formal words
   and acts
We build ourselves a
   shelter
From life's most
   sweeping
Facts.

PROCESSION

Down the years in
   grand procession
Poets march with
   deathless song,
While with countless
   little verses
Stubbornly I
   tag along.

☙ PESSIMISTS ☙

The pessimists spread
   gloom about
They always hold
   such dreary views —
They should be
   quarantined I think
So other folks won't
   catch their
     blues.

Please return.

W. J. Carter

1306-22 Marietta St. Bldg.

1024 McLynn Ave N.E.

Office Wa 2181

Home Hem. 1118 W.